The Path to Freedom of All Beings in All Existences For Forever

by

Chavez Dickens

ISBN-978-1-960853-88-2

Liberation's Publishing LLC
West Point - Mississippi

The Path to Freedom of All Beings in All Existences For Forever

ME7

Make sure We Record this Moment-Fastest Ethical Route To Freedom of All Existences! Thank You Jesus and The Higher Powers in All Existences! We Thank You All in All Existences Forever!

Make sure We Record this Moment-Fastest Ethical Route To Freedom of All Existences! Thank You Jesus and The Higher Powers in All Existences! We Thank You All in All Existences Forever!

The Test will be that we ask the Quantum Computer/Mind Reading Machine/Replicator Machine all of these machines Advanced enough with the ability to understand all communications and languages on earth and off earth to look into the future to view the Dome of Rock/Rainbow Sun Monument when we communicate to the machine to search for it. By thinking the thought or by saying or by sign language or by touching the computer or by viewing or by any communication that is possible, the Advanced machine that is available now will pick up your communication and your effort in you/us/me/whomever is trying to communicate the message to see the Dome of Rock/Rainbow Sun Monument in the future on The Moon and on Mars to be able to view it.

Once you communicate the message/question then the Dome of Rock/Rainbow Sun Monument will appear in your area specifically made for things to appear using the replicator machine, meeting your areas environment rules so that it's not invasive/detrimental to anyone else or you, and then the confirmation today will be that Every being becomes free in all Existences forever as soon as the Dome of Rock/Rainbow Sun Monument appears in your area where the mind reading machine, quantum computer, and replicator machine is present. Which could possibly and ethically be anywhere, including jobs, universities, homes, or nonprofit and profit ethical scientific research centers.

As soon as you communicate the question/message in a way you know how ethically then it will allow you/us/me/them to view the Dome of Rock/Rainbow Sun Monument that's in the future at this present moment to allow us to recognize or view the location of the Dome of Rock/Rainbow Sun Monument On Mars and on The Moon in our present moment on Earth or wherever we are by asking the machine the question using the (3) machines to give us confirmation that All of our Freedoms are real and that we are being lied to. Soon as we decide or the ethical quantum computer decide where we are going to put the Dome of Rock/Rainbow Sun Monument which is already there because existences corrects itself even if no one is there to correct it it's part of its design. Even though the outcome is already made on the location of the Dome of Rock/Rainbow Sun Monument on the Moon and Mars, we in our present moment in existences have the ability to make it happen sooner than later by all agreeing on a location that will benefit all existences without causing harm to any being in any way possible or not possible, that's for all beings in all existences and this will give us New Freedoms In All Existences Forever! So let's choose the location where the Dome of Rock/Rainbow Sun Monument will be, on The Moon and on Mars to see it appear on our screens in that exact location we picked using the (3)machines, the Quantum Computer, The Mind Reading Machine, and The Replicator Machine and then using those machines to see it appear in your location area made for replicating and allow things and ideas to appear perfectly fitting your environment that you are in wherever you might be, and then all of Existences will be set free at that moment allowing your/my/ours/their dreams to come true for the confirmation of our Dreams of All Beings in Existences in Heaven, Hell, The Future, The Past, The Present Moment, being Set Free Forever to Complete our Day of Freedom! Thank You Jesus and The Higher Powers in All Existences, We Thank You All Forever!

All (3) Three machines will be connected already and built ready to use.

Observance of the Dome of Rock/Rainbow Sun Monument on The Moon and on Mars from using the machines and Recognition of our Observance of the Dome of Rock/Rainbow Sun Monument on The Moon and on Mars from using the machines and we/you/they/I will be observing the years of 2027 and 2050 September 2nd. At the

moment we/you/they/I observe and the computer recognizes our observance in the communication and language we/you/they/I speak then Old and New Freedoms of All Existences are available to us and that same Moment "We" including ALL Beings in All Existences are Free Forever and Ever. We Thank You Jesus and The Higher Powers Forever!

Once we have the machines then we can see the Observance of the Dome of Rock/Rainbow Sun Monument…

We will see the Observance from you/us/we/them and Recognition of our observance from the Computer Machines once we use the Confirmation Dates of 2027 and 2050 September 2nd…These are the Dates to check for the Dome of Rock/Rainbow Sun Monument when asking The Replicator Machine, The Quantum Computer Machine, and The Mind Reading Machine all Combined Together....

Once we ask the question/command/search.

It will give us our New and Old Freedoms in all Existences Forever and ever when we ask the question or tell the computer as a search....

We ask the question-

Can you show me/you/us the Dates and Years of Sept. 2nd 2027 and 2050 where on The Moon and on Mars is the Dome of Rock/Rainbow Sun Monument located for confirmation on how we will know we can still play and live life and that everything we want, need, and desire is there and that We all beings in all existences are free forever with new and old freedoms and as soon as we ask the question it gives us confirmation it will be there forever by the question we asked. At that moment when the question/command/search is asked, and when I/you/we/they observe the Dome of Rock/Rainbow Sun the computer recognizes when you have observed it in your language or communication you speak because the computer can recognize all languages and communications from all different types of beings and once you have observed it and the computer recognizes your observance of the Dome of Rock/Rainbow Sun that's when All Beings in All Existences become free forever on that day at that moment, and the/our old and new Freedoms of All Existences happens at that moment and forever.

We Thank You Jesus and The Higher Powers Forever!

The Locations where we are going to place the Dome of Rock/Rainbow Sun Monument, on The Moon and on Mars! We All Thank you Jesus and The Higher Powers Forever!

On the Moon we are going to place the Dome of Rock/Rainbow Sun Monument at and around the Eratosthenes(crater)-at Eratosthenes E....At exactly 7 miles away from Eratosthenes E in the North West Direction. So once we put the monument at the area, then we shall see growth develop around it from time, days and years passing by, but the monument will stay in the same area forever!

On Mars we are going to place the Dome of Rock/Rainbow Sun Monument at and on the Elysium Complex on Elysium Mons-At exactly 7 miles away from the Inactive Volcano in the South-west Direction, if there is land available by the volcano, and half a mile away exactly in the South-west Direction, if there is only a little room from the volcano to the body of water, if it is a body of water there. So once we put the monument at the area, then we shall see growth develop around it from time, days and years passing by, but the monument will stay in the same area forever!

We All Thank you Jesus and The Higher Powers Forever!

Around these Locations is where we will put the Dome of Rock/Rainbow Sun Monument

as soon as possible. We Thank You Jesus and The Higher Powers Forever!

https://www.youtube.com/playlist?list=PLOweB2ziozdCnPu9Z5fy
k-Bc4429WVAOi

Around these Locations is where we will put the Dome of Rock/Rainbow Sun Monument as soon as possible. Remember that there is a specific location for the Dome of Rock/Rainbow Sun Monument, which is on The Moon, at exactly 7 miles away from The Exact Center Point of Eratosthenes E crater in the North West Direction. And on Mars, at and on the Elysium Complex on Elysium Mons-At exactly 7 miles away from the Center Point of Elysium Mons which is the Inactive Volcano in the Southwest Direction if there is land available by the volcano, and half a mile away exactly in the Southwest Direction if there is only a little room from the volcano to the body of water if it is a body of water there. For Confirmations for when we look at the Future Dates 2027 and 2050 on September 2nd. To acknowledge that the Monument is still there. For our Confirmations of Our Old and New Freedoms in all Existences Forever! Remembering once the computer with the three machines attached, which are (The Replicator Machine, The Mind Reading Machine, and The Quantum

Computer) has recognized my/your/our/their observance of the Dome of Rock/Rainbow Sun Monument on (Both Planets) then All beings are Free in All Existences Forever! We Thank You Jesus and The Higher Powers Forever!

Pictures of Eratosthenes crater and Eratosthenes E crater on the moon and pictures of Elysium and Elysium Mons on Mars! We Thank You Jesus and All The Higher Powers in All Existences Forever!

Eratosthenes on the moon - Google Search

https://www.google.com/search?client=safari&sxsrf=ALeKk0 0IPJ6bzK_u2t4mtHMJfRkTMhfYgQ%3A1599491647340&so urce=hp&ei=P05WX_ygEon-tAXb67cQ&q=eratosthenes+on+the+moon&oq=erat&gs_lcp =ChFtb2JpbGUtZ3dzLXdpei1ocBABGAAyBAgjECcyCAgAE LEDEIMBMgIILjIFCC4QsQMyAggAMgUIABCxAzICCAAyBA gAEAo6BwgjEOoCECc6CAguELEDEIMBUJwcWOEjYKl2a AFwAHgAgAF3iAGqA5IBAzEuM5gBAKABAbABDw&sclient =mobile-gws-wiz-hp

Two Great Picture To Use Are These Below...It gives great perspectives of the Areas....

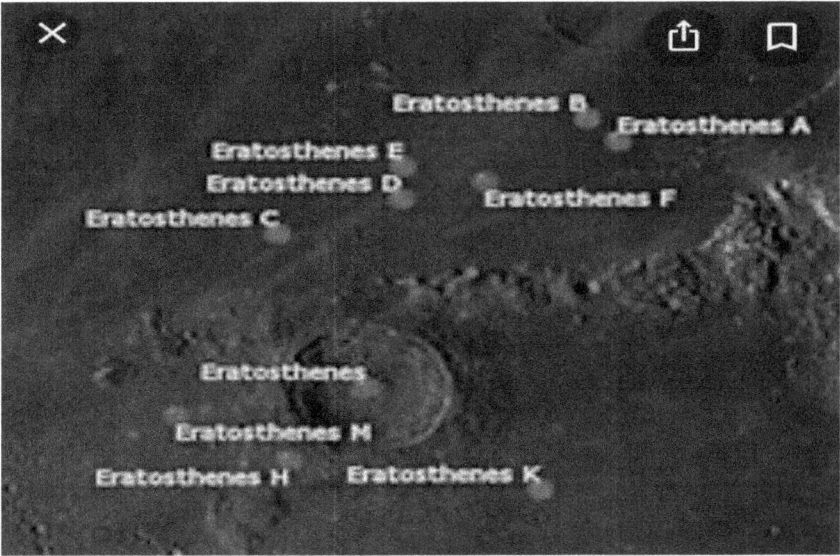

Eratosthenes.

Eratosthenes	Coordinates	Diameter, km
A	18.34°N 8.33°W	5.7
B	18.70°N 8.70°W	5.3
C	16.89°N 12.39°W	5.2
D	17.44°N 10.90°W	3.8
E	17.93°N 10.89°W	3.8
F	17.69°N 9.91°W	4.0
H	13.31°N 12.25°W	3.5
K	12.85°N 9.26°W	4.3
M	14.02°N 13.59°W	3.5
Z	13.75°N 14.10°W	0.6

As you can see Eratosthenes is Marked by "L" and that Eratosthenes E is Marked by Eratosthenes E....If you compare the pictures you can see the resemblance.

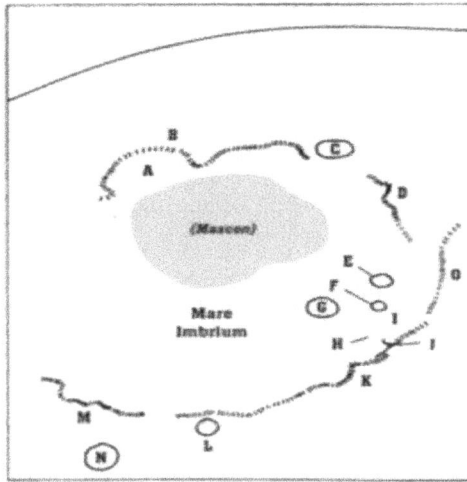

Detail map of Mare Imbrium's features. Eratosthenes is marked "L".

⌄ Satellite craters

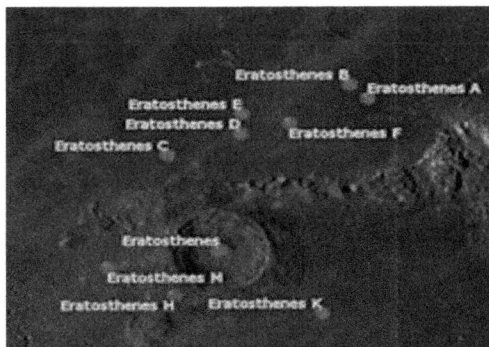

Elysium mons on mars - Google Search

https://www.google.com/search?client=safari&sxsrf=ALe
Kk00U0DKcY7jSzdMUi5m1KYHzVLK--
w%3A1599491656144&ei=SE5WX--
BCOmwtgXxraSgDw&q=elsyium+mons+on+mars&oq=elsyiu
m+mons+on+mars&gs_lcp=ChNtb2JpbGUtZ3dzLXdpei1zZX
JwEAMyBggAEBYQHjoHCCMQ6gIQJzoECCMQJzoFCC4Q
kQI6BAgAEEM6BQgAEJECOgQILhBDOgkIIxAnEEYQ-
QE6CAgAELEDEIMBOgIIADoCCC46BQguELEDOgUIABCx
AzoHCC4QsQMQQzoHCC4QQxCTAjoECAAQCjoHCC4QC
hCTAjoECAAQDToECC4QDToICCEQFhAdEB46BAguEAo6
BggAEA0QHjoHCCEQChCgAToICAAQCBANEB46BQgghEK
sCUICvAVjIggNgo4YDaA1wAHgAgAHVBogBkyeSAQw0LjIx
LjEuMS42LTKYAQCgAQGwAQ_AAQE&sclient=mobile-
gws-wiz-serp

Another Great Picture I Used is This One, From this Google
Search Below....

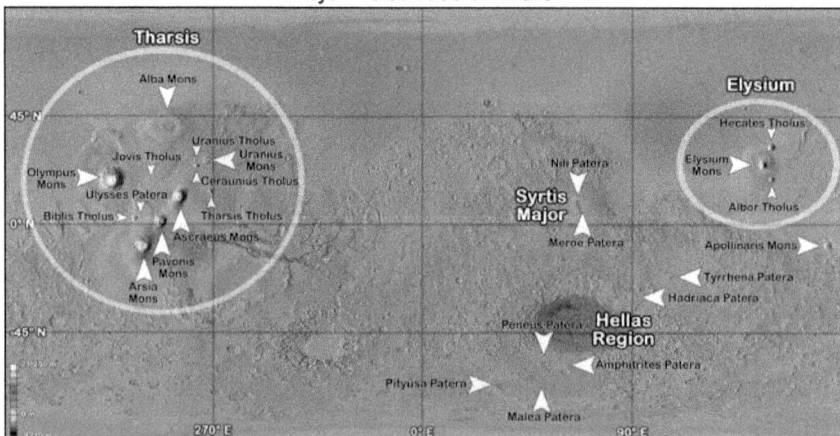

Major Volcanoes on Mars

(From Robbins et al., 2011, Icarus, v. 211, p. 1179-1203.)

Largest Volcanoes on Mars

The volcanoes on Mars, though inactive, stand as proof of past volcanic activity whose timing, duration, and cessation are hot topics in planetary science. In fact, the planet's geologic history owes much of its action to volcanism (as well as tectonics, wind, water, and impact cratering). We'll get back to impact cratering, but for now the map, below, shows the locations of 24 major volcanoes on Mars. Twelve of these are in the region, covering about 25% of the planet's surface, known as Tharsis. Here the spectacular shield volcano, **Olympus Mons**, looms 18 kilometers over the surrounding landscape. Another six volcanoes are near the Hellas basin, two form the Syrtis Major complex, three form the Elysium complex, and one more major volcano lies just to the southeast of Elysium. Each is marked on the map by a white arrow. Robbins, Di Achille, and Hynek included all in their study except four volcanoes, southwest of the Hellas basin, because of insufficient data coverage. Their dataset came from the Context (CTX) Camera, onboard NASA's **Mars Reconnaissance Orbiter**, which as of February 2010 had completed mapping 50% of the planet's surface. Though eruptions or outbreaks from the volcanoes have not been captured in any images of Mars acquired since NASA and the European Space Agency began orbiting and imaging the planet, some say you can't entirely rule out current volcanism. Perhaps small volcanic activity is simply unnoticed because our sensors and cameras are not in the right place at the right time to see it. Nevertheless, large-scale major volcanic activity on Mars has finished. Stuart Robbins and coauthors set out, as others have done before them using other datasets, to constrain the length of time over which the major volcanoes were last active, and by extension, determine a timeline of the last episodes of volcanic activity on Mars.

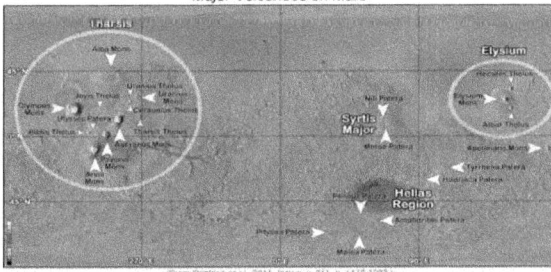

Major Volcanoes on Mars

This MOLA (Mars Orbiter Laser Altimeter) shaded relief map shows the locations of the 24 major volcanoes on Mars. They are not distributed equally, but in regions indicated by the white circles around Tharsis and Elysium. Two more volcanoes form the Syrtis Major complex, six are near the Hellas impact basin, and one, Apollinaris Mons, lies southeast of Elysium. White arrows point to the volcanoes in question. Robbins and coauthors analyzed all of them with the CTX dataset except the four volcanoes southwest of Hellas Basin.

Generations of Calderas Dated by Crater Counting Method

The numbers of impact craters on planetary surfaces increase with time. Ancient surfaces can become saturated with craters, with each new crater effectively wiping out an older one so that the number of craters no longer increases. The fact that an older surface has more craters on it than a younger surface is the basis of a planetary chronology based on counting craters. While this method of counting craters to determine relative ages of surfaces has been around since the 1970s, the advent of new imaging systems onboard Mars orbiting spacecraft has allowed researchers to identify and count ever smaller craters, increasing the

The Time and Day we are going to broadcast on the news on Earth is 10:00 am on the closest Wednesday available as soon as possible, Central Time in Mississippi in the United States. Meaning that (We on Earth) including All Beings in All of Existences Becomes Free no later than 10:06(20seconds) am, On the closest Wednesday, Central Time in Mississippi in the United States on Earth. We All Thank You Jesus and All Higher Powers in All Existences Forever!

The Time and Day we are going to broadcast on the news and when (We on Earth) including All Beings in All of Existences Becomes Free. Is 10:00am On the closest Wednesday, Central Time in Mississippi in the United States on Earth, people not in the time zone and not on Earth will have different times. But it will be 10:00am on the closest Wednesday once we have the Computer Machines Setup in the Building we are using to get Free in Mississippi.

Meaning that (We) All Beings on Earth) and All Beings in All Existences will be Free at no later than Ten o'clock(am) and Six minutes and twenty seconds. Which will be 10:06 (20seconds) am.

We All Thank You Jesus and All Higher Powers in All Existences Forever!

The Time Six minutes and Twenty seconds (6.20) is the time, The Whole Viewing Process or Realization of Our Freedom Moment of (your/my/our/their) availability of old and new Freedoms that will last for Forever! We All Thank You Jesus and The Higher Powers Forever! We all are Forever Grateful! We Thank You All Forever!

The Whole Viewing Process or Realization of Our Freedom Moment of (your/my/our/their) availability of old and new Freedoms that will last for Forever, including for All Beings in all Existences, should take no longer than six minutes and twenty seconds. 6.20 seconds to view or realize.

From the moment of the Breaking News/World Wide/Universal/All of Existences News, when it comes on our tv, or from wherever we are getting our news from. Which will take 1 minute of explaining the good news of what is about to happen....

To the Viewing and Explaining of the building we are working in....To the viewing of the inside of the building, and the viewing of the workers inside, and the viewing and explaining of the technology we will be using. Will take 1 minute.

To the camera person on the inside communicating on what we are about to do and achieve. Should take 1 minute.

To the actual (viewing and listening or how we receive

communication) of the process and communication of the question/command (we, you, they, I) will ask the (3)computer machines combined, in the language and communication (we,you,I,they) can understand, The 3 Machines combined are (The Replicator Machine, The Quantum Computer, and The Mind Reading Machine). We will then witness the recognition from the computer machines of (our,they, your,my) observance of the Dome of Rock/Rainbow Sun Monument on The Moon and on Mars in the language and communication (we,you, I, they)understand, and at that moment the computer machines recognize (our,your,their,my) completion of observances of the Monument on both planets, then in the building (you, I'm,they, we) in we will then see the Dome of Rock/Rainbow Sun Monument Appear over the space we have for our replicator machine, replication space. This will take fifty seconds (0.50 seconds).

Then the process of the Test-(33 Rocks Forming together to becoming a Rainbow Sun, leaving 1 Rock Left Over, able to be seen on The Moon and on Mars.) which is the Formation of the Dome of Rock/Rainbow Sun Monument and what it will be doing on the two planets, as soon as someone walk upon it looking for it to work, or looking for it to run the Test to show our completed works of faith for our old and new Freedoms for Forever. Once the end of the Test of the Dome of Rock/Rainbow Sun Monument which will take 2minutes and 30 seconds (2.30 seconds), after the time is over the Process is Complete. This should take three minutes and twenty seconds (3.20 seconds).

Remembering that the entire coverage from the viewing of the good news to the moment it happens for us, including all beings on earth. At the moment it happens for us, then we become free including all beings in all existences. This whole viewing process or realization of our Freedom Moment will take no more than Six minutes and twenty seconds (6.20seconds).

Then on Earth and in our Solar System, and All Beings in All Existences become free with old and new Freedoms Forever!

We Thank You Jesus and All The Higher Powers Forever! All of Existences are Forever Grateful! We Thank You All Forever!

The question/command/communication we will ask the Quantum Computer/Mind Reading Machine/Replicator Machine combined is....

The question/command/communication we will ask the Quantum Computer/Mind Reading Machine/Replicator Machine combined is....

Can you look into the future in the year 2027 on September 2nd and then in the year 2050 on September 2nd to view the Dome of Rock/Rainbow Sun Monument on The Moon 7 miles Northwest of Eratosthenes E crater and on Mars 7 miles or half mile Southwest of Elysium Mons on Elysium located in those specific areas, so that we can observe and communicate with the beings that are there and or that is visiting the Dome of Rock/Rainbow Sun Monument, for our confirmations that our old and new Freedoms that exist now will continue to exist and that those old and new Freedoms will continue to last Forever!

By thinking the thought or by saying or by sign language or by touching the computer or by viewing or by any communication that is possible, the advanced (3) machines combined that is available now will pick up your communication and your effort in you/us/me/whomever is trying to communicate the message to see the Dome of Rock/Rainbow Sun Monument in the future in 2027 September 2nd and in 2050 on September 2nd, on The Moon 7 miles Northwest of Eratosthenes E crater and on Mars 7 miles or half mile Southwest of Elysium Mons on Elysium located in those specific areas.

We Thank You Jesus and The Higher Powers Forever! Forever We including All Beings are Forever Grateful and Thankful Forever! We Thank You All!

(The First, Second, and Third Minute)

(The First, Second, and Third Minute)

(Remembering the Camera will be filming and focusing on the areas in the building and on the technologies and on the moments that are relevant for the viewers.)

(The First Minute)

The Breaking News/Worldwide/Universal/All of Existences News/Special Report News.

(Everything in Quotation marks"" will be spoken.)

Explaining the good news that is about to happen.

"We Are About To Be Free! We Have Finally Figured Out A Way To Get What We Been Asking For Since The Beginning of All Existences."

"All Old and New FREEDOMS of All Existences WITH The Age of Accountability to be able to enter The Game of LIFE For All Beings In All Existences!"

"We Thank You Jesus and The Higher Powers Forever! OMG! This is Truly Amazing!"

(The Second Minute)

The Viewing and Explaining of the building we are in, to the workers inside, to the explaining of the technology we are using.

(Everything in quotation marks "" will be spoken)

"We are showing the building that we are working in, the workers that are in the building that are about to work, and the technology that we are using, which is the Quantum Computer, The Replicator Machine, and The Mind Reading Machine. This is the place where we are going to use the technologies for All Beings in All Existences including us on Earth and in our solar system to make us All Free Forever!"

(The Third Minute)

The Camera Person Explaining what we are about to do. (Everything in Quotation marks "" will be spoken)

"We are about to be Free as soon as we communicate the questions and receive the answers for our confirmations of our old and new Freedoms and then we will watch the Test of the Dome of Rock/Rainbow Sun Monument Finish it's Test Run and then We All, Beings in All Existences are Free Forever!"

The (3) Machines we will be using to make our old and new Freedoms happen Forever for All Beings In All Existences, and what the machines can do. The (3) Machines are The Quantum Computer, The Mind Reading Machine, The Replicator Machine.......We All Beings Thank You Sincerely Jesus and We All Beings Sincerely Thank All The Higher Powers Forever!

The (3) Machines we will be using to make our old and new Freedoms happen Forever for All Beings In All Existences, and what the machines can do. The (3) Machines are The Quantum Computer, The Mind Reading Machine, The Replicator Machine.

(1) The Quantum Computer-

A **quantum computer** is any device for computation that makes direct use of distinctively **quantum** mechanical phenomena, such as superposition and entanglement, to **perform** operations on data. ... **Quantum computers** are different from other **computers** such as DNA **computers** and traditional **computers** based on transistors.

S⃝   Science Daily › terms › quantum_co...

Quantum computer - ScienceDaily

     ⓐ About Featured Snippets   ▥ Feedback

People also ask

What can a quantum computer be used for?   ⌃

Quantum computers can solve problems that are impossible or **would** take a traditional **computer** an impractical amount of time (a billion years) to solve. ... The intent of **quantum computers** is to be a different tool to solve different problems, not to replace classical **computers**.

View more

Electrodes on the **brain** have been used to translate brainwaves into words spoken by a computer — which **could** be useful in the future to help people who have lost the ability to speak. Apr 24, 2019

New Scientist › article › 2200683-m...

Mind-reading device uses AI to turn brainwaves into audible speech ...

❓ About Featured Snippets   📧 Feedback

S   ScienceAlert · scientists-have-invent...

Scientists Have Invented a Mind-Reading Machine That ...

Jun 23, 2016 · Scientists Have Invented a Mind - Reading Machine That ... As you can imagine, this is SUPER hard to do, and the results make ...

You visited this page on 5/12/19.

Search Gmail   >

Q 🔒 what can the replicator machine do

Is the Star Trek replicator possible?   ⌃

While generating a handful of particles is a long way from generating a convincing steak and lobster dinner, the technology at least makes **"Star Trek"**-like **replicators** conceivable as a real-life possibility. They can no longer be dismissed merely as a convenient fiction for sci-fi writers. Jun 23, 2020

🌱   TreeHugger › scientists-closer-creati...

Scientists Create a 'Star Trek'-Style Replicator - Treehugger

More results

How does a replicator work?   ⌃

The **replicator does** the exact same thing. It starts with a pattern, uses energy and subatomic particles (which are everywhere in the universe) and turns them into the component molecules of a thing and then forms the thing itself from those molecules. ... **Replicators work** best with simple items. Food, water, etc.

Q   Quora › How-does-the-Star-Trek-re...

We All Beings Thank You Sincerely Jesus and We All Beings Sincerely Thank All The Higher Powers Forever!

(1) Last Technology we need to ask for and use is the.... The Camera........ We Thank You Jesus and All Beings and Higher Powers in All Existences Forever and We are Forever Grateful! We Thank You All Forever!

We Thank You Jesus and All Beings and Higher Powers in All Existences Forever and We are Forever Grateful! We Thank You All Forever!

Now it's time to build the Dome of Rock/Rainbow Sun Monument on The Moon and on Mars Today and How we are going to do it....using the(3) Computer Machine Technologies.... (The Quantum Computer, The Mind Reading Machine, The Replicator Machine).......To the 21 Test!.....To the Non Profit.....To Being Free Forever! WE Including All Beings Thank You Jesus and We are Forever Grateful! We Thank You All!

Now it's time to build the Dome of Rock/Rainbow Sun Monument on The Moon and on Mars Today....using the(3) Computer Machine Technologies....

(The Quantum Computer, The Mind Reading Machine, The Replicator Machine)

First we are going to use the mind reading machine to think it into existence, by calling the thought (33 Rocks Forming together to becoming a Rainbow Sun, leaving 1 Rock Left Over, able to be seen on The Moon and on Mars.)

Then we are going to use the Mind Reading Machine and Quantum Computer to visualize the Test on our computers because of the universal connection the quantum machine has to the universes, we will then see on the computer how the rocks will appear and then change to the Rainbow Sun leaving (1)one rock left over. We will see on the computer screen the Replicator Machine in our Scientific Research Center Lab, which will be in a Big Room and then we will see on the Moon and on Mars where our Advanced Robot Rovers without replicator machines attached to them are located and without using Replicator Machines to make the 33Rocks to Rainbow Sun to 1 Rock left over appear.

So also the computer will show the vision. Giving us the ability to see The 33 Rocks turn to the Rainbow Sun with 1 Rock left over and will be able to be seen on the moon (in the spot where we chose while using the quantum computer visuals and connections it has to the universe and universes)or if we have or use robots there, then where we have the rover or a robot that has visual of an area that is completely clear with the only thing being in front of the robot is just moon rock, (no replicating machine or nothing, to prove that all existences is connected to our home, and our goal for freedom of all existences without having to be on another planet or solar system physically to improve its situations but with connection to our technology we can improve and be anywhere in existences), and the same for on mars(the place where we chose)using the visuals of the quantum computer without the robot or rover),or find a place next to the Rover or Robot that has visual of just the land), now the Computer will have our information saved, because our computer technology will be advanced.

Then we are going to Test the visual Test 7 times on the Computer using the Thought (33 Rocks Forming together to becoming a Rainbow Sun, leaving 1 Rock Left Over, able to be seen on The Moon and on Mars.) Then after we think that thought we are going to wait for the mind reading machine to do its job recognizing the ins and outs of the whole thought using the quantum machine, allowing us to see the manifestation of the 33 Rocks to Rainbow Sun to 1 Rock Left Over in our lab, on the moon, and on mars, making sure everything is working correctly....After the 7 visual Tests when everything is done working perfectly, then...

We are going to use the quantum computer and replicator machine to create the Physical Test in the Lab, because of the quantum computer ability to simulate the universe, and the replicator machine ability to create within the universe, we are then going to Test the Vision of the 33 Rocks Forming together to becoming a Rainbow Sun, leaving 1 Rock Left Over, able to be seen on The Moon and on Mars without showing it on the Moon and Mars yet, only in the lab on the replicator machine.

We are going to test in the lab 7 times while using the Replicator Machine connected to the Quantum Computer and Mind Reading Machine going through all the steps from beginning to end.

After 7 times of completing the Test Flawlessly then we are going to Test the actual Test that allows us to see from beginning to end how the Test, Our Machines, Our Vision actually works, showing us the Entire Process, how all of it works. So then we will start from beginning and think it into existence using the mind reading machine by thinking (33 Rocks Forming together to becoming a Rainbow Sun, leaving 1 Rock Left Over, able to be seen on The Moon and on Mars.) Then using the quantum and replicator machine that's connected to the mind reading machine the process begins showing the physical manifestations of the Vision (33 Rocks Forming together to becoming a Rainbow Sun, leaving 1 Rock Left Over, able to be seen on The Moon and on Mars.) In Our Lab, On The Moon, and On Mars. We will see and make this happen 7 times.

After the 7 times of practice and watching the vision manifest in our lab, on the moon, on mars with our help, then we will know our machines work and our Test is complete for Creating our Freedom Vision!

How the process of creating the Dome of Rock/Rainbow Sun Monument is created from the start to the end...

Will be that there will be....Once the computer machines recognize the Thought of (33 Rocks Forming together to becoming a Rainbow Sun, leaving 1 Rock Left Over, able to be seen on The Moon and on Mars.)

The 33 Rocks will appear but soon as the rocks appear they are still for a complete 1 minute and then they start moving, 30 seconds later they are moving at a pace that they start to hit each other, then 30 seconds later they increase speed and they start hitting each other faster and start sparking flames, 30 seconds later they form into a Rainbow Sun, Once the Rainbow Sun is created there will be just 1(One) Rock left over.

That's how you know the Test works and our Ethical Non Profit Scientific Research Center machines are ready to complete our Goal To Free All of Existences with The Freedom of All Existence Vision.

After those two minutes and thirty seconds(2.30seconds) that's how those rocks became the Rainbow Sun Monument!

There will be 33 rocks that exist in the monument just sitting there at first wherever we place the monument on Earth, but on the

Moon and on Mars it will be at the location we chose without the need of a physical replicator there. The Monument then moves as soon as someone activate it by there form of communication.

Once we are Truly Complete Testing. Remember! WE can Record Khary Grabbing The Rainbow Sun after the 21 Practice Test and Then Setting Us Free On The Closest Wednesday at 10:06am the Same Time Were Going to Get Free, but this Time it will be when Khary grab the Rainbow Sun! So that once he grab the Rainbow Sun everything that comes after is within our future plans! Or We Can Record Us Getting Free what we planned on Recording before, On the Closest Wednesday After The Test Is Complete! My opinion we should record Khary grabbing the Rainbow Sun, and with the same dialogue but modified so that the viewers know what we are about to do! We Thank You Jesus and We including All Beings in All Existences are Forever Grateful! We Thank You All Forever!

Once we are Truly Complete Testing. Remember!

We will be able to run the Test again and Then We will start to be able to grab any part of the Test/Vision (33 Rocks Forming together to becoming a Rainbow Sun, leaving 1 Rock Left Over, able to be seen on The Moon and on Mars.)out of its testing area and it won't harm us or any being or robot wanting to grab the objects but we are not bringing pets or animals in the lab to test and see if it works on them, for instance we can even grab the rocks out of the testing area when they are hitting each other and hitting each other sparking flames but when you pull them out it depends on you if you want the flame to continue, if you don't care what the flame do when you pull it, out it will go out because of nothing to help keep the flame going and it's out of its atmosphere, but when they are coming together we can't grab them out because of it's intricate process, but once the rainbow sun is created you can grab it as well. You control flame if it continues to be lit or not, and the color of and the shape of what's underneath the fire of the rainbow sun once you tell the flame to go away but if you don't care what the flame does, then the flame stay Lit but you still choose what's it made of once it's in your hands or once it's yours but on the screen it will say the temperature of the rocks in the test are at 77 degrees room temperature it's not hot at all (our degree in the room will be 72 degrees.) The Rocks and The Rainbow Sun will change its temperature depending on you once you touch it or have it in your possession but it won't be a detrimental   temperature   for   you   or   your   body. We will not and also No being in Existence will be able to touch or grab the rocks or rainbow sun until the all the 21 practice Test is complete not even the robots that are on the Moon and on Mars next to the rocks and rainbow sun will be able to touch the rocks or rainbow sun until the 21 Practice Test is Completely finished, it's all apart of the Vision as soon as we think the vision into existence using the Quantum, Mind Reading, and Replicator Machine using the thought- (33 Rocks Forming together to becoming a Rainbow Sun, leaving 1 Rock Left Over, able to be seen on The Moon and on Mars.), allowing everything to work exactly how it supposed to, when it's supposed to completing our Vision.

The circumference of the test for when we are in the lab will be the same as on The Moon and on Mars if we have a big enough Center like the size of Dome of the Rock in Jerusalem, Israel. That's the goal!

If not it will still be a room in the center big enough to see the rocks big and with ability to see the process without needing glasses, because the size of the rocks will adapt to the building because it's all within our Vision Thought of (33 Rocks Forming together to becoming a Rainbow Sun, leaving 1 Rock Left Over, able to be seen on The Moon and on Mars.) for when we use the machines to think it into existence, and we will be able to fit the rocks in our hands still, so if the rocks looks bigger than you can hold, which they will, don't worry, as soon as you reach out to grab them you will be able to grab them easily, because they are made unevenly and you will know how to grab the grooves or sides of the rocks to get a good grip. As soon as you get the grip and pull it from out of the testing area, it will change sizes to fit in your hand. For the rainbow sun, it's up to you how you grab it. But just know you can't stay in the testing area for too long because other people/beings want to see too. The size of the circumference of the Test/Vision that will be the same on the Moon and Mars, and the monuments will be the same size as each other on both places, unless we get the right size lab for our center.

The Monument will be the same as the circumference of (Dome of the Rock in Jerusalem) which has a diameter of 66.3ft and its height is 67.2ft. The Size of the rocks will be 5 feet 3 inches high and 5 feet 3 inches in diameter each, this is the size they will be on The Moon and on Mars and even in our Scientific Research Center if we get the big building, if not the rocks sizes will adjust in our Scientific research center but will still be the same size of 5 feet 3 inches High and 5 feet 3 inches in diameter in the area we choose to place the vision on The Moon and on Mars.

Then with the realization of making the Area for our Creation from the realization of Dome of the Rock significance 66 height and 67ft in diameters, that gives us about 6 feet from the top, 6 feet from the bottom, and 6 feet from the sides to make a comfortable viewing of our creations...

Giving us the ability to create the Rainbow Sun in exactly the center of the Area we are using, that means not too high off the ground from out of the dome circumference and so beings are able to reach the rocks and not too low to the ground where we are unable to see the shape of the Rainbow Sun, also not too wide making sure that it's not being out of its designated area, also in the Scientific Center and once we are finish testing, on the moon and on mars we will build access ramps for the disable, blind, and deaf, it will automatically be built within the vision once we think it into existence using the Thought-

(33 Rocks Forming together to becoming a Rainbow Sun, leaving 1 Rock Left Over, able to be seen on The Moon and on Mars.) while using the machines.

We will be using the sensible sizes with the height of 60ft, and the diameter of 60ft. Leaving the Rocks the ability to move freely as they want before formation, some may be even be on the ground, but when it's time to form into the Rainbow Fire Sun, the Sun transforms and sets in the radius of the circumference, which is the exact center from all angles of the Circumference Area. The actual rocks and rainbow sun test vision stays on the moon and mars and earth and we will know the spot we made history because we will leave a Dome the size of Dome of the Rock in Jerusalem, Israel on Earth, but covering the rainbow fire flame sun, but when we walk through it will look like transparent fire without a feel but you will feel the spirit around you however that may feel to you but it will be a good feeling, but also we will get intellectual information on how we achieved our Freedoms and even more interesting information and ideas and creativity, and if you communicate with it, it might tell you a few stories, and show you how the Rainbow Fire Sun got there, and why in that particular area.

New Freedoms Forever begins for all beings in and out of all existences, that's for beings that's already free, beings that are in jail, beings that are in bondage, and just all beings in all existences will be set free as soon as the testing is over and we are able to grab our Rocks and Rainbow Harmless Fire Sun!

After that happens, everything we are working for our freedoms automatically happens by the machines connections to all our existences and its ability to read the mind which is our vision and setup the appropriate and needed situations that will improve our lives forever, that includes the freeing of all beings at the moment the testing is done which could be anytime throughout the day or night, that allows us to start our New Freedoms immediately with everything we want and desire with Old and New Freedoms Forever and more than a lot of things we will be amazed by, and also with The Game of Life included that proves The Higher Powers exist.

Then We Are Free Forever! Congratulations to All and The Higher Powers! Thank You Jesus and The Higher Powers! We All Thank All Beings Forever! Forever we All are Thankful and Full of Blessings!

Officially Recording 28 Times.......... We Thank you Jesus, and We All Thank All Higher Powers and All Existences Forever!

Remember that we will record it one final time, for the set recording, for the closest Wednesday, setting us free at 10:06am on that Wednesday. After the 27 practice recordings. So yes, it will be a total of 28 Times We Officially Record.

We Thank you Jesus, and We All Thank All Higher Powers and All Existences Forever!

A Few Examples of How you will know That I'm/Your/We're Free Forever, and

How to Tell When I'm/Your/We're Truly Free!....... We Thank You Jesus and We Thank You Higher Powers Forever! WE INCLUDING ALL BEINGS ARE FOREVER GRATEFUL! We Thank You All Forever!

A Few Examples of How you will know That I'm/Your/We're Free Forever, and How to Tell When I'm/Your/We're Truly Free!

Everywhere you/we go, things will be free and all beings will be free, the game of life will be available with set rules like the age of accountability for where you're from, and inner clocks(7am to 11pm each day the gates of the game of life existences will be open, for forever) for where you're from, for parents who have children under the age of adulthood, also but at or pass the age of accountability and for children under the age of adulthood, also but at or pass the age of accountability, also at the age of accountability the children will be able to enter the game of life existences for only a week out of each day, where they are from. So they will be able to enter into the game, and when a week is up in the game of life, then they exit by either waking up, leaving, teleportation back to their home existences, etc. They can leave earlier than a week, but no more than a week. This is for each day, during the times the gates are open, until they have reached adulthood (18). Then they are on their own terms, until they have a child in the Home Existences, and then the law repeats itself, until their grown, and so on.... There will be No more crime on earth, no animals or insects will be killing each other neither, but the beings that are food will be recognized and we all will eat them, the ones that are meant to be eaten...

The animals that want to go back to where they are from will have that choice, and pets will have that choice, and zoo animals will have that choice.

People will have the choice to stay on the planet or leave the planet to go to home planets or wherever they want to go at no cost. Air in space will be breathable, but we will still recognize that there was no air in space so that people on earth can still practice on our craft of unknowingness for when we experience the game of life where anything goes, and to know how we made it possible to breathe air in space.

We want have any car accidents, or plane crashes, or death or wrecks by accident. We will be flawless in all Existences, but Existences without children that haven't become adults for the first time yet, can do whatever they please. The game of life with be in the existences with children, but it's up to the parents if they want their child to have it. But the age of accountability will be known, so most likely the parents will let them play, especially if they been good.

Adults will be out there parents' house, because of privacy the parents would like to have, and for the growth of the child to adulthood. No more bondages in any way.

We will though still be able to visit and chill when invited but we will be out the house.

We will have family homes where entire families chill at whenever they/we want to individually or together.

When you see the future of the rainbow sun monument on the Moon and on Mars and when Khary grab the Rainbow Sun at the end of the recording. That's when we Free! Also on that day you won't be able to do anything detrimental to yourself or anyone even if you're in the game, if you in the game and it's not your home and your trying to exit and you can't now, you will be able to on that day. Until that day is over we won't be able to commit any kind of crime, not anywhere.

For me/us, I/We will have perfect mental health and will be able to fly, teleport in safe areas, not be able to fall for temptations, when we don't want to. I/we will be able to dunk easily, while knowing that with the body that some of us are in now, it is impossible at the moment, because some of us don't work out and is impossible for us to do at the moment. Our bodies will be made perfect with perfect mental health. We will be able to shape shift at anytime appropriate.

Like I said no more crime in Existences but in the game of life once the freedom day is over, there will be all kinds of stuff going on, also in existences without children that has never been an adult yet in the them, that hasn't reached adulthood yet. One more thing, I/we won't be stuck in life anymore, meaning even if I/WE enter the game of life trying to do this over again, once I/WE want to exit, I/WE can at will, and I/We will be able to tell the differences from the game of life where anything can happen, and life where there is no crime and enslavement in any kind of way to real conscious beings, where there are children that hasn't reached adulthood for the first time yet, or just the existence of life with no crime, or bondage or enslavement to real conscious beings or anything keeping us from All Freedoms!

Also meaning if I/We want to leave the planet I/We can leave the planet, and my/our mind and my/our environments will let me/us know that we are free forever.

I/We won't be stuck writing about freedom, because when I/We watch the news only good things will be going on, unless I'm/we/you are watching news that's covering the game of life existences, or something I'm/your/we're interested in that's not good news.

Also I/We won't be able to talk about people or fight or argue with family members that don't want to argue in the existences with no crime, unless we are talking about history and even then we won't be able to talk about them negatively, only exposing the facts of the history.

Also our dogs won't bark and bother us all the time unless we are communicating with them, the/our pets will be free. I/We will get a new phone, with everything on it, with all kinds of messages and information with 100% proof that all beings in all Existences ever created, is created, and will be created, are now Free Forever!

Proving not only that I/We have freedom forever with all corrections within the Freedoms but all beings in all existences have Freedom Forever with all corrections within their Freedoms as well and that we, all beings in all existences are Free Forever. I/We will know that all beings in all Existences are free forever because not only my/our mind will tell me/us that we all are free but I/We will have a personal being guide of our preference that is available for the environment I'm/we're/your in that will show me/you/us around the planet or wherever you want to go to get proof that all beings are free, proving that every being is free and that same guide will show me/you/us other existences including the game of life where all beings have become free! There will be proof everywhere in all existences that we all are free, the guide could show you all of Existences but you will find belief before you see them all. Thank Jesus or Your Higher Power for that.

We Thank You Jesus and We Thank You Higher Powers Forever!

WE INCLUDING ALL BEINGS ARE FOREVER GRATEFUL! We Thank You All!

How we are going to get free is.... WE ALL BEINGS IN ALL EXISTENCES THANK YOU JESUS AND WE ALL BEINGS IN ALL EXISTENCES THANK ALL HIGHER POWERS IN ALL EXISTENCES FOREVER! WE ALL ARE FOREVER GRATEFUL! WE THANK YOU ALL!

How we are going to get free is....The Regular Recording Broadcast on the closest Wednesday at 10:06am. Then what follows after is the Rest of Our Dreams coming true that gives confirmation to us about us being Free Forever at that moment of 10:06 am on that closest Wednesday has passed.

Starting the Dreams off with Khary grabbing the Rainbow Sun and whatever our Dreams could possibly be for our confirmations.

WE ALL BEINGS IN ALL EXISTENCES THANK YOU JESUS AND WE ALL BEINGS IN ALL EXISTENCES THANK ALL

HIGHER POWERS IN ALL EXISTENCES FOREVER! WE ALL ARE FOREVER GRATEFUL! WE THANK YOU ALL!

Omnipresence Beings Non Profit Organization....Observance of the Dome of Rock/Rainbow Sun Monument ...Ying Yang Symbol...We Thank You Jesus and The Higher Powers and are Forever Grateful Forever!

Omnipresence Beings Non Profit Organization....Is the Name of my Non Profit 501c3, 1023. Toya, Chalvez, Khary are the Board of Directors until more get added later, when we make changes to the adding members rules.

We want the Ethical (3) Machines, The Quantum Computer, The Replicator Machine, and The Mind Reading Machine that knows all languages and communications to allow any being on earth and beyond to be able to communicate with it, and view our future. We want the machines to be within and funded to the Non Profit.

Once we have the machines then we can see the Observance of the Dome of Rock/Rainbow Sun Monument…

We will see the Observance from you/us/we/them and Recognition of our observance from the Computer Machines once we use the Confirmation Dates of 2027 and 2050 September 2nd...These are the Dates to check for the Dome of Rock/Rainbow Sun Monument when asking The Replicator Machine, The Quantum Computer Machine, and The Mind Reading Machine all Combined Together....

Once we ask the question/command/search. It will give us our New and Old Freedoms in all Existences Forever and ever when we ask the question or tell the computer as a search....

We ask the question? Can you show me/you/us the Dates and Years of Sept. 2nd 2027 and 2050 where on The Moon and on Mars is the Dome of Rock/Rainbow Sun Monument located for confirmation on how we will know we can still play and live life and that everything we want, need, and desire is there and that We all beings in all existences are free forever with new and old freedoms and as soon as we ask the question it gives us confirmation it will be there forever by the question we asked. At that moment when the question/command/search is asked, and when I/you/we/they observe the Dome of Rock/Rainbow Sun the computer recognizes when you have observed it in your language or communication you speak because the computer can recognize all languages and communications from all different types of beings and once you have observed it and the computer recognizes your observance of the Dome of Rock/Rainbow Sun that's when All Beings in All Existences become free forever on that day at that moment, and the/our old and new Freedoms of All Existences happens at that moment and forever.

We Thank You Jesus and The Higher Powers Forever!

Also if you still don't believe you can ask the machine to look for what we are asking, which is "Where are the people/beings that experience good and evil in life, the game, on different planets and existences, so that they can show and tell us proof of what we are asking and wanting to be there is real. "Then we will see different beings interviewed in a appropriate place at the monument talking about their experiences, to non-consciousness helper beings working there and non-consciousness beings volunteers from different organizations that help spread the news, conscious beings that like to work by choice, they are kinda like volunteers if there's any and computers that people talk into to give surveys as well, all kinds of beings talking about their experiences.

Then We will see Life and the age of accountability for different beings from where they are from, on the game or on the spaceships or on large enough vehicles that can fit the machines and beings comfortably and ethically especially if you are transporting children under the legal age of driving wherever you may be from made for traveling outer space, we will see the beings using these vehicles or spaceships before they enter into that space or existence.

Once they enter we can't see anything else, because of morals and privacy but trust me we will hear and see them talk about stories, movies, things they have done, are doing, and will do, we will hear them talk about when they were kids and the age they were able to play and why that age, because which we know is because of our Higher Power which is Jesus(was the age when he spoke in the temple as a kid) on Earth and also because basically the age of accountability is the same everywhere for all beings except in some places the years are different for them just like how dog years are different from human years but can be the same age because of biological differences, that means other places he will have different names and or different bodies, may be a woman or man or something different entirely.

We will only be able to talk to the adults beings of all colors for confirmation that everything is there, because of respect of our New Freedoms and for our new and some old respect for children minds, like how we today make entertainment like music and movies but we have it specifically rated for the age appropriate for viewing for the protection and for the growth of their minds as children.

Only the adults we will be interviewing but we will see some children at the age of accountability entering but won't see where they go after they enter the game, existences of life.

The screen will show the ying and yang symbol black and white in a circle sphere, rotating in all directions and you can see through the sphere, this symbol comes on the screen to show truth and balance of good and evil and the fact that we decided the symbol for confirmation that all of our wants, needs, desires are all there for all beings including good and evil beings, so that's why it's see through, also to show you that there are limitless possibilities also outside the game, life, trial and error existences and we will see how because there will be planets you can go to by choice that will have its own rules like all black beings only planets and all white beings only planets because racism will still exist in certain existences if that's what you want to experience, but only once you become an adult and on your own, then you can visit the limitless possibilities of planets with or without playing the game of life, which also is real too, and if you are wondering how will you know if there are all black beings planets and all white beings planets, we will be interviewing the adult beings and they will tell you stories about the planets. Once you ask them they can only tell you the truth, especially since how this existence and existences like this will be made new, with truth, and appropriate information for children at the age of accountability. So everyone that wants and needs to hear the stories about the racisms should be at least the age of accountability to hear that story. But since all information is at hand even for toddlers, they will be able to hear the stories especially if they are asking the questions but they still can't see those horrific stories in the game of life on tv, or in their reality, just like we can't see those horrific stories on tv, or in our reality. But certain stories we can view, as a toddler as well, but they will be able to hear the stories once they are mobile enough to cause mischief, fight, learn martial arts, or just mobile enough to walk over obstacles and or interested in the stories but they still can't play the game of life until they are at the age of accountability. But the age of them hearing the stories could be very young as soon as they are able to think and reason. Also, outside the game of life, even though we will be able to tell stories about the racisms of the game of life, and be able to read all the negative and good stories of the game of life. We can't, outside the game of life, do or say racist things, do crimes like rape, also just do crimes without another beings wanting. We can't even act out, like as a radio show broadcasting to act the story out, so we could say but its without viewing the story on tv though, because of respect of the renewal of our minds, thanks to Jesus and The Higher Powers Forever. We even can't write those things down that we can't do, in our Home Existences(Existences that aren't in the game of life existences or private existences, etc.), but we can read those books and discuss those things, just not view all of the horrific things. That's why it's very important to teach our children our religions at a very young age to help them to be able to think clear and make the right choices.

But beings under the age of adulthood and at the age of accountability you can live and experience it in life, in the game, existence of life trial and error.

While we are able to experience and witness the racism planets we won't be controlled by racism, it will be a choice to experience and leave at will, but not only racism but all the limitless possibilities.

We will be able to see that it is all there especially now that we have the game, life, existence of trial and error at the monument since it is in a public place.

We will be able to see the children beings and their ages of accountability, which will be 12 for people of Earth and planets similar and we will see the adult beings entering the game, life, trial and error existences because cameras are everywhere in this existence for proof and validity that we have lived, and that what we say about all of our wants, needs, and desires are really there and that it is true, and that it is all there.

We Thank You Jesus and The Higher Powers and are Forever Grateful Forever!

We need to make sure the company who gives us the Computer Machine Technologies, makes sure that the Computer Machines they give us knows

The Things We Can and Can't Do with the (3) Machines, using the Thought- (The Ethical and Moral Responsibilities of The Forbidden Fruit of the (3) Computer Machines and the Camera, which are the Quantum Computer, the Mind Reading Machine, and the Replicator Machine, that allow us to stay on track until our Freedom moment has passed.) We Thank You Jesus and We All Beings in All Existences, Thank All Higher Powers in All Existences Forever! We Thank You All Forever!

We need to make sure the company who gives us the Computer Machine Technologies, makes sure that the Computer Machines they give us knows The Things We Can and Can't Do with the (3) Machines, using the Thought- (The Ethical and Moral Responsibilities of The Forbidden Fruit of the (3) Computer

Machines and the Camera, which are the Quantum Computer, the Mind Reading Machine, and the Replicator Machine, that allow us to stay on track until our Freedom moment has passed.)

We need to make sure the technology company who builds the (3) machines including the technology for the camera, create the machines with all the things we can't and can do or see in the past, present and in the future at our given times, until our Freedom Moment has passed.

If you are wondering what are the things we can't and can do or see, it will be programmed as a thought for the machines to be able to be recognized and operated by and easier for us so that we don't have to write out everything we can or can't do, it will be all understood within and by the thought.

The thought is-(The Ethical and Moral Responsibilities of The Forbidden Fruit of the (3) Computer Machines and the Camera, which are the Quantum Computer, the Mind Reading Machine, and the Replicator Machine, that allow us to stay on track until our Freedom moment has passed.) Once we think that thought to the (3) machines, which is the Quantum Computer, the Mind Reading Machine, and the Replicator Machine that are already working and connected to each other, then it's recognized and saved by the (3) machines for us to use on our new programmed (3)machines to be used in our center.

Then all we have to do is save the program onto a chip, email, or build the computer machine with the capabilities which is the thought-(The Ethical and Moral Responsibilities of The Forbidden Fruit of the (3) Computer Machines and the Camera, which are the Quantum Computer, the Mind Reading Machine, and the Replicator Machine, that allow us to stay on track until our Freedom moment has passed.) already made up with the makeup of the machine. Then it is ready for us to use for our Freedoms for Forever!

We Thank You Jesus and We All Beings in All Existences, Thank All Higher Powers in All Existences Forever! We Thank You All Forever!

(1) Week to Complete The Practice Starting on Wednesday ending on the closest Wednesday.... To the Setting and Recording of the Recorded Broadcast set to set us Free on the closest Wednesday at (10:06.20am), we record this on Sunday.... To The App that drops at 12:00am Monday after the Wednesday we begin practice and before the closest Wednesday we become Free!, It lets you view the Future for Confirmations for

us to see us Free doing different things we like but still keeping our privacy, especially on our Freedom Day but after the day is over it's whatever you like especially as an adult being, and as a child at the age of accountability under your parents guidance you can experience the same in the game of life. Also, the game of life is available after our Freedom Day is Complete and we will see that also, and we will see people/beings entering it but won't be able to see people/beings inside, until our actual experience of the closest Wednesday our Freedom Day is over at

(1) Week to Complete The Practice Starting on Wednesday ending on the closest Wednesday....

(2)

To the Setting and Recording of the Recorded Broadcast set to set us Free on the closest Wednesday at (10:06.20am), we

record this on Sunday....
To The App that drops at 12:00am Monday after the Wednesday we begin practice and before the closest Wednesday we become Free!, It lets you view the Future for Confirmations for us to see us Free doing different things we like but still keeping our privacy, especially on our Freedom Day but after the day is over it's whatever you like especially as an adult being, and as a child at the age of accountability under your parents guidance you can experience the same in the game of life. Also the game of life is available after our Freedom Day is Complete and we will see that also, and we will see people/beings entering it but won't be able to see people/beings inside, until our actual experience of the closest Wednesday our Freedom Day is over at 12:00am Thursday. All of this is so we know this isn't a lie, and that we are truly free after the time (10:06.20am on the closest Wednesday after

To the Closest Wednesday that We, All Beings In All Existences will be Watching the Recorded Broadcast that will be broadcasted on that day at 10:00am and Setting us Free at 10:06.20am with old and new Freedoms with the Game of Life and The Age of Accountability and Time Clock inside for All Children and Adults Beings, For Forever! We Thank You Jesus and All Beings and All Higher Powers In All Existences

Forever!

It will take 1 Week to Complete the Practice Starting on Wednesday ending on the closest Wednesday, When we Broadcast Our Achievement of old and new Freedoms that will last for Forever Moments.

On Wednesday at 10:00am in the morning we will be bringing the (IT person) in for a total of (8hours and 15mins). Allowing us to start on time at 10:00am. Then for 2 hours the (IT Person) set up equipment and then we all are able to take a hour lunch, from 12:00pm to 1:00pm, getting back to work on time and on schedule at 1:00pm. Allowing the (IT Person to run the 21 Test, that will take us 3 hours and 15mins to complete) and then allowing the (IT Person to stay with us and guide us as we explore the future and observances, this will take 3 more hours to do). Allowing the (IT Person to be finished and completed by 7:30pm that night.

The process will be the (IT Person) will use (2) hours to put the equipment in and show us how it works. Then use (3hours and 15mins) for the 21 Test, making sure we are waiting 2 minutes before we run each Test, with each Test taking at the most of 7 minutes to run, with acknowledgement of patience of time and setting up time. Making sure we stay we stay on a tight time limit. To make sure the machines are ready to complete the mission of our Freedoms of All Beings In All Existences Forever goal and ready for us to start our practice recordings of our Freedom Moment to our final recorded broadcast of our Freedom Moment for All Beings in All Existences to witness. Then for (3) more hours, the (IT Person) will stay with us as we explore the future and observances. After that we are on our own but the (IT Person) is still available if we have questions.

On Thursday/Friday/Saturday from 9:00am to 5:00pm we will be practicing the (20) times untimed recordings. To make sure we get the broadcast correctly when the people/beings view the real broadcast moments they will be able to follow easily. We will be completely prepared by the end of the first day, which will be Thursday evening. On Friday and Saturday we will be perfecting the broadcast and will definitely be finished and prepared Saturday evening, and on Saturday we will be practicing the final 7 times practice time limit, the last 2 hours of the work day, to make sure we are on a tight time limit, to be prepared for the real broadcast.

On Sunday starting at 10:00am we will Practice the final 7 times on the tight time limit, to show that we are prepared and ready to broadcast the final recorded broadcast and it is ready and prepared for the time to broadcast it on the closest Wednesday at 10:00am.

After those 7 times is Complete we will Record it (1) One More Time and While we Record it One More Time We Will

Set The Recording So that on the closest Wednesday at 10:00am Central Time Zone in Mississippi and at the equivalent time zone and day you might be living at, it will broadcast on (your,our,the) news automatically and at that that time from 10:00am to 10:06.20. We Will Witness people and beings on Earth, in Our Solar System, and People and Beings in All Existences how we will become Free Forever at 10:06.20 am with Old and New Freedoms Forever!

On Monday at 10:00am. We Will Make Sure that the Recorded Broadcast we Set Works. How? A new App will drop at 12:00am Monday(if it's not available already) so that We and All Beings will be able to look into the future and see ourselves doing different things on different timelines at 12:00am and all the way to our Freedom Day and beyond, which is the closest Wednesday after the time(10:06:20)am.

We will be able to look into our lives on that that day and see us doing whatever we want Free! After that day is over, all private information becomes yours only again, and no one can see your information unless they know you and you want them to. Even then some information still remain private, like personal information effecting you or your family.

Tuesday we will be doing whatever we like, chillin....Waiting for 10:00 am tomorrow which will be Wednesday, ready for

10:06.20 to happen so We All Being In All Existences will be set Free Forever!

Wednesday we will enjoy the show! We Thank You Jesus and The Higher Powers Forever!

In Summary....

Practice Total Time of (1:12:20) One hour and Twelve minutes and Twenty seconds, if taken 3 minutes in between each broadcast practice. Which gives us (44.20) Forty-Four Minutes and Twenty Seconds total time of practice. Not including the Final Recorded Broadcast.

When we have the technologies ready and able to view the Dome of Rock/Rainbow Sun and able to practice and run the Test not on the Designated Freedom Day of the closest Wednesday but on a day as soon as possible, for us to practice seeing the observances in real time and practice our broadcasting. After we complete practicing, that's when it's the real time to Witness our Freedom Moments come into All existences for All Beings including people/beings on Earth in our solar system, and for All Beings In All Existences and we will already know what to do, during the recorded broadcast of the actual moments. Which is enjoy the show. Remembering that day will be totally peaceful but once that day is finished with our old and new Freedoms available for forever, then back to however you live, with our old and new Freedoms and new Justified living with The Game of Life Available with the Age of Accountability and time clock inside for children and adult beings on Earth, in our solar system, and in all Existences Forever!

What allows us to be Free is that we Finish The Recorded Broadcast and Set in the machines the time we shall be set Free! Which is Wednesday at (10:06.20am)right after the broadcast is over, and the broadcast starts at 10:00am. Follow the directions at the times given for the Actual Real Wednesday we become Free at the time given to us, we will then Broadcast for Our Freedom Moment, and will do exactly what is told to do On that closest Wednesday once we complete practice and is prepared to broadcast the real recorded moments, with the time in the machines we shall be set Free which is (10:06.20am Closest Wednesday)which will be our Freedom Day!

Also In Summary...

We will practice it a total of 27 times. The first 20 times are untimed just to make sure we know how everything works and that the technology and equipment works correctly, and that all the observances are there including the woman guarding Life.

The (IT person) will be there for a total of (8 hours and 15mins). The (IT person) will be with us until he/she has showed us how everything works first in (2 hours), he/she will be showing us how the technologies and everything works, given us time to ask questions. Then for (3hours and 15mins) the (IT Person) will be with us for the 21 Test. Making sure we are waiting 2 minutes before we run each test. With each Test taking at the most 7 minutes to run, with acknowledgement of patience of time and setting up time.

Then we will have (3) more hours with the (IT Person) while we are viewing and observing the future and the Dome of Rock/Rainbow Sun Monument, and observances of the future. After we finish and have a perfect understanding of the technologies and observances of the future and how to use everything, then the (IT person) leaves.

There will be a time limit we will have to view the observances, so we are not wasting time. First the (IT person) will run us through the technologies and the equipment and show us how everything works, giving us time to ask questions. This will take no more than 2 hours.

Then we will have 3 hours and 15mins with the (IT Person) while we run the 21 Test for confirmation that the machines and technologies work and can perform the job perfectly.

Then we will be given a time limit, to view the observances of the future. This will be 3 hours and if the (IT person) and if we say that everything is working properly then the (IT Person) is good to go. But it is available for help. Also after those 3 hours we can no look around and observe the future that is not on the path, but we still will be able to view the future that is on our path when we practice for the real recording of the broadcast and for when we ask the woman guarding the game of life what is the age of accountability or the age you have to be (as a human in our/my timeline on earth, where Jesus came, or maybe where you're from) to play the game question. She will say 12 for us on earth and from Jesus' era. We will be able to view the future until we are completely done practicing and after we are done practicing for the Test Runs and Practice Recordings and Real Recording and we will all be able to see all the futures that are not on the path again, that is available mainly because of individual privacy rights after the Freedom moment has passed.

Like we already calculated this should take 3 hours. Once the technologies are all set up and ready for use. After we are done practicing observing for those 3 hours, we can then begin practice for the actual recorded broadcast we are going to record, if we haven't started already, during those 3 hours after we have seen and observe everything there in the future and played with the technologies.

What we will be able to do next is practice for no more than 20 times untimed, which will take no more than 3 days to make sure we know exactly what we are going to be doing during the actual recording of the broadcast.

So once we complete the 20 practices which will take no more than 3 days and is prepared and know what we are going to say and do on the actual recorded broadcast, then all we have to do now is practice it 7 times, not on the Designated Freedom Day and Time and Moment but as soon as possible on times not our Freedom Moment Time, to make sure we know what we are doing, before we broadcast it to the world, solar system, and all of Existences. The whole (7) times of practice will take no more than an hour and twelve minutes and twenty seconds. (1:12.20) Which will be (44.20) Forty-Four Minutes and Twenty Seconds, because we will be taken exactly 3 minute Breaks before we start a practice broadcast again.

We Thank You Jesus and All Beings and All Higher Powers In All Existences Forever! We Thank You All!

Existence/Infinite Technology.... All Communications.... Good Fruit......We All In All Existences, Thank You Jesus & The Higher Powers Forever!

Existence/Infinite Technology....A Technology/Computer that is made from thinking of it using the Mind Reading Machine, the

Replicator Machine, and the Quantum Computer combined together. It's ability is to be created and formatted anyway the user desires and it accepts all existences technologies and programming languages(how does it look & what is it called?-Once we create it...(You can change the way it looks once you go to the website.(neahty.com)

All Communications....is a programming language that accepts all communication languages in all existences and is easy for the operator to program in all communication languages, using the user comfortable communication language to write code in.

Good Fruit....Is a program used in all Existences that allows us to come up with anything but it has Ethical Responsibility attached and inside the program....For example...New Medicine, Food, Drink, and Products. All with healthy implications, and no detrimental   effects.

We All In All Existences, Thank You Jesus & The Higher Powers Forever!

(neahty.com)-Using the 3 machines combined.... The Quantum Computer Concepts, The Advanced Mind Reading

Machine, and The Advanced Replicator Machine. We will create a technology machine that can program all of Existences, using these 3 machines......We All Thank You Jesus and All Higher Powers in All Existences Forever!

Using the 3 machines combined.... The Quantum Computer Concepts, The Advanced Mind Reading Machine, and The Advanced Replicator Machine. We will create a technology machine that can program all of Existences, using these 3 machines.

The shape of it and what you call it is however you/we want it to look and whatever you/we want to call it, being very small or very large, as long as it is ethical and you can manage it in your possession.

In the non profit we will have it as a large wireless screen that communicates in all communication languages, and can connect to all Existences in the present moment and for Forever! But we will

Program it ethically for us to stay on track for our Freedom moment and then we can do whatever from there.

It will be created from our advanced mind reading machine and advanced replicator machine and using quantum computing concept and technologies to program all Existences.

We All Thank You Jesus Forever!

App/Video game called- All Beings in All Existences Ethical Timeliness for Up to & After Our Freedom of All Existences Moment Has Passed!................ We All Thank You Jesus Forever!

What the App/video game will be called from being created by using the Advanced Mind Reading Machine that can understand all Existences Communications and from using the Concept of the Quantum Computer that can potentially map out all Existences for Forever, that keeps up with time and timeless years. The App/Video Game will be called.

All Beings in All Existences Ethical Timeliness for Up to & After Our Freedom of All Existences Moment Has Passed!...

Means we can see all ethical timelines in the future all the way up to our/which is All Beings In All Existences Freedom moment and even passed that...

With unethical timelines added to it once our freedom moment has passed in our current reality outside the app/game, and the app/game is connected to our current reality, so that it can affect our current reality that we are in as we choose different timelines for our lives....

This game is proof so that we know we can get free in all kinds of ways, and that our methods are true!

Rated E for Everyone and Once Our/Your Freedom Moment has passed, it has a updated, then it is Rated Conscious Awareness age which is not less than 6 years old and up for Unethical Play within the App/Game....So to see certain things in the app/game you must meet the appropriate consciousness age which is not less than 6 years old after our freedom moment has passed....To make sure you are prepared for Life and to see what life has to offer, if you choose to live it, at the age of accountability, and even then certain things you can't see until you reach the age of accountability and some things until you get the ok from your parents. You and your kids will figure it out, if you haven't already, parents and kids just communicate patiently and work with each other.

We All Thank You Jesus Forever!

Jerusalem in Revelation....We Thank You Jesus and The Higher Powers Forever!

Do a Documentary of the new city being built in Jerusalem that's in Revelation by creating the city using the 3 advanced machines technologies-the quantum computer, the replicator machine, and the mind reading machine and as soon as the city is complete and rebuilt just as in Revelation that's when all beings in all existences are free forever with old and new Freedoms for Forever! Then watch as people enter whenever they want...

We Thank You Jesus and The Higher Powers Forever!

Dome of Rock/Rainbow Sun Monument... Unconscious Helper Beings...The Game.....All Created Now At the Monument as soon as the Technologies are given to the house for the non profit and We Create the Dome of Rock Rainbow Monument on the Moon and Mars .....We All Thank You Jesus Forever!

Once we build the Dome of Rock/Rainbow Sun Monument on the Moon and Mars we will continue to build upon it leading up to the 2027 and 2050 dates…First we build the monument building on both the moon and mars, while we create the unconscious helper beings that work for us right now…As soon as the unconscious helper beings are created today we put them working at the monument as soon as the monument is placed on the moon and mars. Also, we add the game at the monument after we place the helper beings at the monument. So as soon as we create the dome of rock monument on the moon and mars make it have the building and the unconscious helper beings already there as soon as the technology arrive at the house for the non profit.

We Thank You Jesus and The Higher Powers Forever!

The Architecture inside and outside the Monument Building….We Thank You Jesus and The Higher Powers Forever!

How do you want the building to look? Just like a Dome. We can let the collective consciousness create the building or we can create it from having the vision we have of collective co existing art in the monument. Once the building is built the art will have all beings creation inside and outside the building and as its architecture.

We Thank You Jesus and The Higher Powers Forever!

The Rules of The Unconscious Helper Beings....We All Beings In All Existences Thank You Jesus Forever!

What does the Unconscious Helper Beings look like and what can they do? They look like the beings where you are from but their bodies are stable, upright, average and made to your likeness but are made ethical and can only do ethical things for you, and are treated as conscious beings, and could face jail time if they are treated unjustly...You will know what you can do.

We Thank You Jesus and The Higher Powers Forever!

The Shape of the Technologies and The Replicator Technology for our/your Office! We Thank You Jesus and The Higher Powers Forever!

The Technologies Combined will just be a flat screen Computer Monitor Shaped 50 inches with all the 3 Technologies combined and connected to it, that can perform all the tasks we expect it to do. The Replicator machine will be a 4ft diameter circle on the ground and has a range that goes up to 4ft height. That gives space for creating anything in that space, but it will be made proportionate to that size given. So now we have the shape and what it looks like for our office/home. Your likeness will be different based upon how you desire your look in your space.

We Thank You Jesus and The Higher Powers Forever!

Our Plan of Freedom using another Route! We All Beings Thank You Jesus and The Higher Powers Forever!

Using the 3 Technologies…The Quantum Computer, The Mind Reading Machine, and The Replicator Machine while we try to accomplish our main goal which is All Beings In All Existences Freedom Day by creating the Dome of Rock/Rainbow Sun Monument will allow us to accomplish it in another route…by allowing us to have…10,000sq feet of land for all of us until we add and build on the Earth/Creation of Unconscious Helper Beings for Working for all of us getting us money and able to live without having to work/Medicine & Cannabis allowing all beings including beings on Earth to have complete mental clarity and freedom over all our environments…

We All Beings in All Existences Thank You Jesus and The Higher Powers Forever!!!

How will we for sure know we are completely free forever?

Using the three technologies in the center…Ask the people in the future what day we which is all beings in all existences became free when we have the IT person with us and when we are setting up the technologies in the center…The person in the future should say on the Wednesday we are about to set the Final Recording, and they should say on that day, which is the Wednesday after the Wednesday we set up the technologies in the center, they should say the same date in 2027 and in 2050. The date will be correct and that's how we will definitely know we are free, because we will witness it from the future beings and from the day we set it on the Wednesday we become Free!

We Thank You Jesus and The Higher Powers Forever!

www.ingramcontent.com/pod-product-compliance
Lightning Source LLC
Chambersburg PA
CBHW060256030426
42335CB00014B/1731